The Adventures of ALEX THE PIRATE:

Treasure Island

Tom Oldaker

First published 2023
by Rowanvale Books Ltd
The Gate
Keppoch Street
Roath
Cardiff
CF24 3JW
www.rowanvalebooks.com
Library Cataloguing in Publication Data.
A catalogue record for this book is available from the British Library.

This is
Alex.

Alex has a
great imagination
and loves to play.

Alex always
dreamed of being a
pirate and
searching for
treasure.

However, being a
pirate
isn't easy.

A pirate needs to know
all four sides
of the pirate ship...

Remember to salute when meeting the captain...

And be willing to
lend a helping hand.

The captain and Alex sailed the pirate ship across the seven seas in search of treasure.

IT WAS SO MUCH FUN.

Alex was excited to find treasure on Treasure Island.

Alex helped load it all into the treasure chest and onto the pirate ship.

That's when the naughty pirates
came to try and steal the treasure.

OH NO!

Alex took the chest back to Treasure Island and buried
it to stop them from finding it.

But the naughty pirates kept sailing towards
Treasure Island.

Alex had to
help stop them.

Alex prepared the pirate ship for battle by loading the cannons. Alex fired the cannons and sank the naughty pirate ships.

The captain awarded Alex a medal for being so brave.

Alex loved being a pirate.

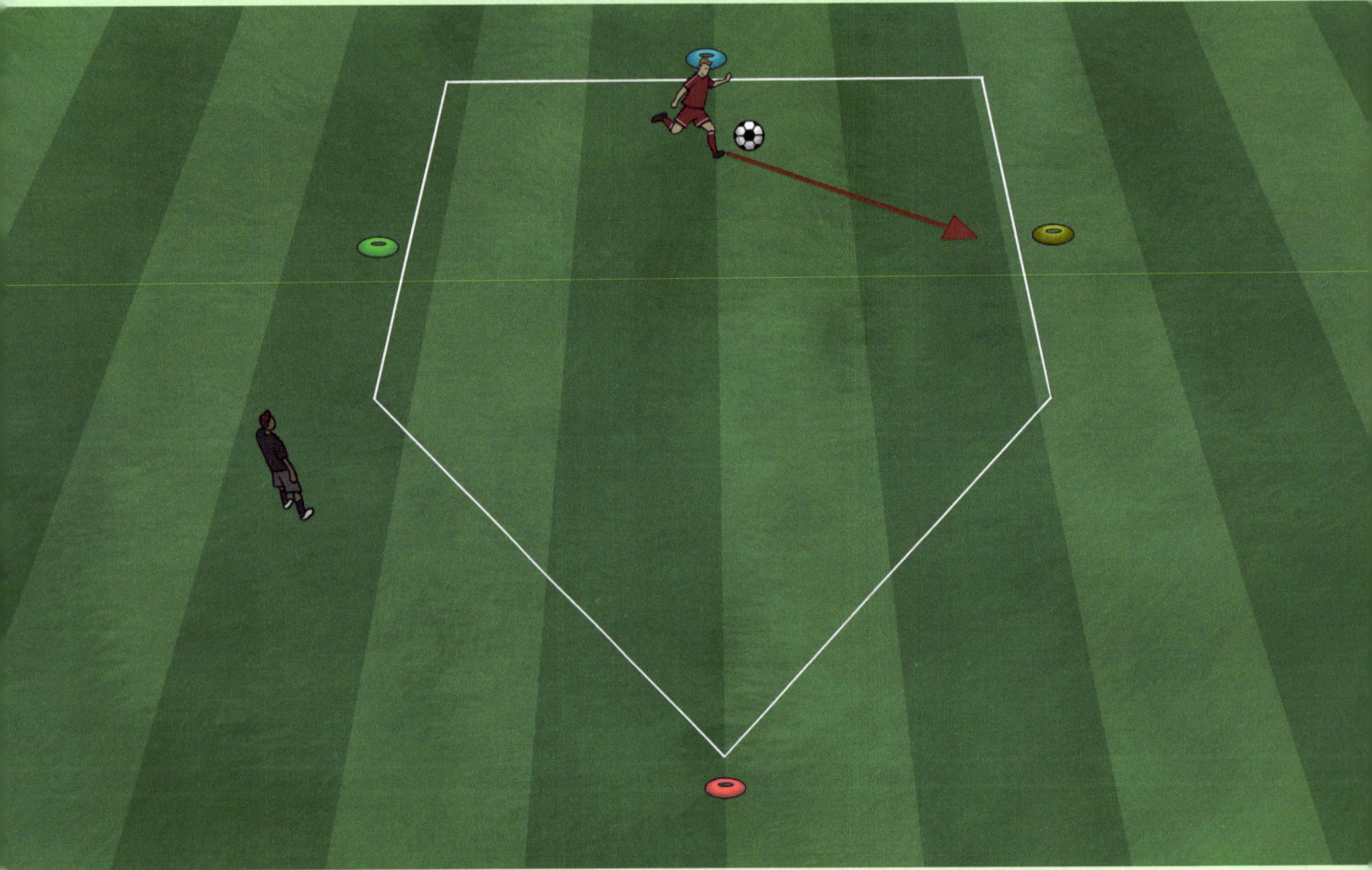

PIRATE SHIP

Organisation of Game

Create a pirate ship using cones.

Use a different coloured cone to represent each side of the pirate ship.

The pirates (children) hold the treasure (balls) in their hands.

The pirates follow the instructions of the captain (adult):

"Bow" = Run to red cone.

"Stern" = Run to blue cone.

"Port" = Run to yellow cone.

"Starboard" = Run to green cone.

"Captain's coming" = Salute the captain and say, "Aye aye, Captain."

"Scrub the deck" = Pretend to scrub the floor.

Progression

Pirates place the balls on the ground and dribble between the cones using little kicks.

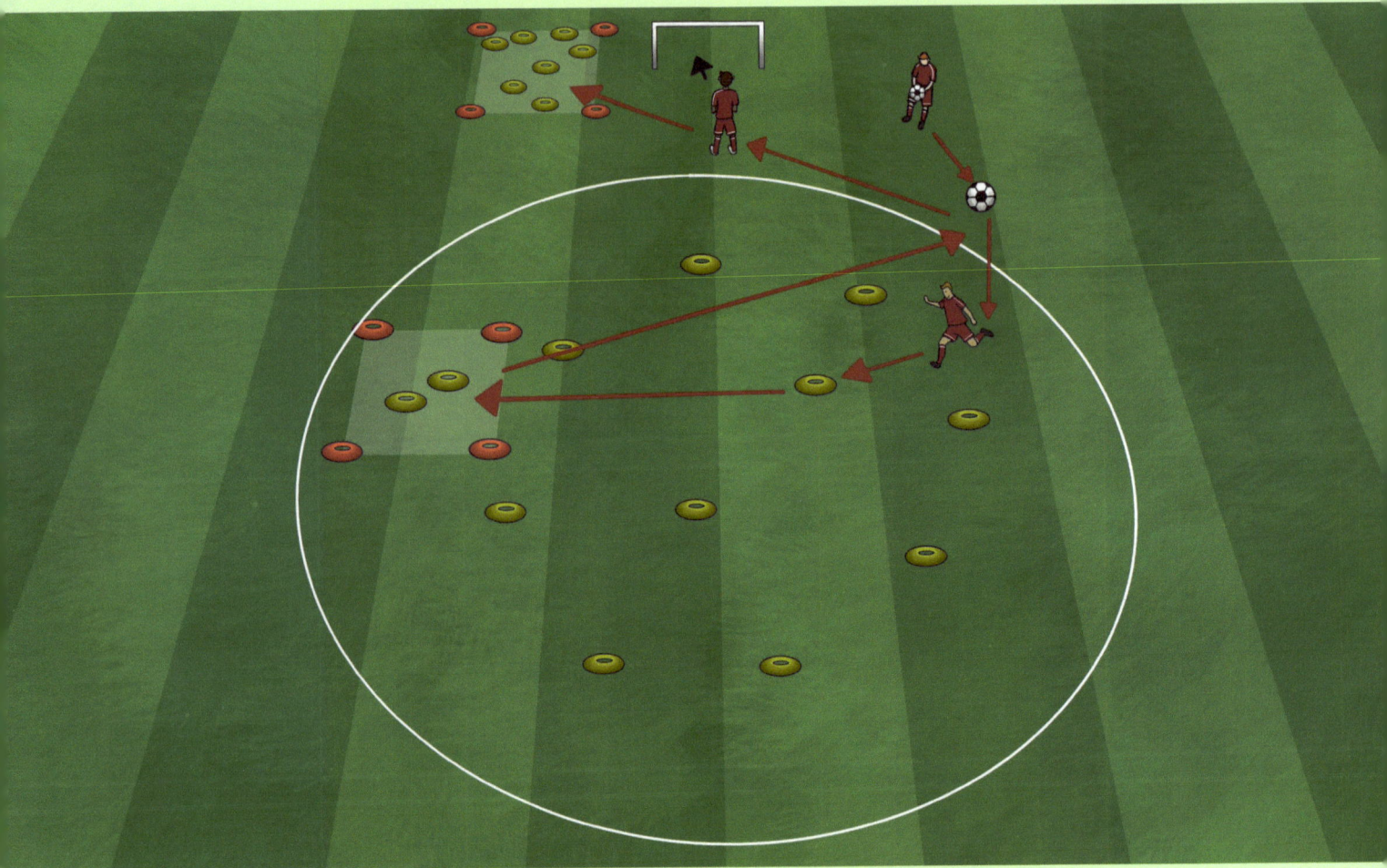

TREASURE ISLAND

Organisation of Game

Create Treasure Island by placing cones in a large circle formation.

Spread out treasure (cones) on Treasure Island.

Create a treasure chest using cones and place it on Treasure Island.

Pirates sail their pirate ships (hold the balls) from the pirate dock (goal) across the ocean to Treasure Island.

Pirates dock their pirate ships (place the balls on the ground) and climb onto Treasure Island.

Pirates collect one piece of treasure (cone) at a time and place it inside the treasure chest (coned area).

Once all the treasure has been collected, pirates take the chest back to their pirate ships (carry all cones).

Pirates sail their pirate ships back to the pirate dock (kick the ball into the goal).

Pirates place the treasure chest (cones) next to the pirate dock (goal).

Progression

Pirates place the balls on the ground and dribble across the ocean using little kicks.

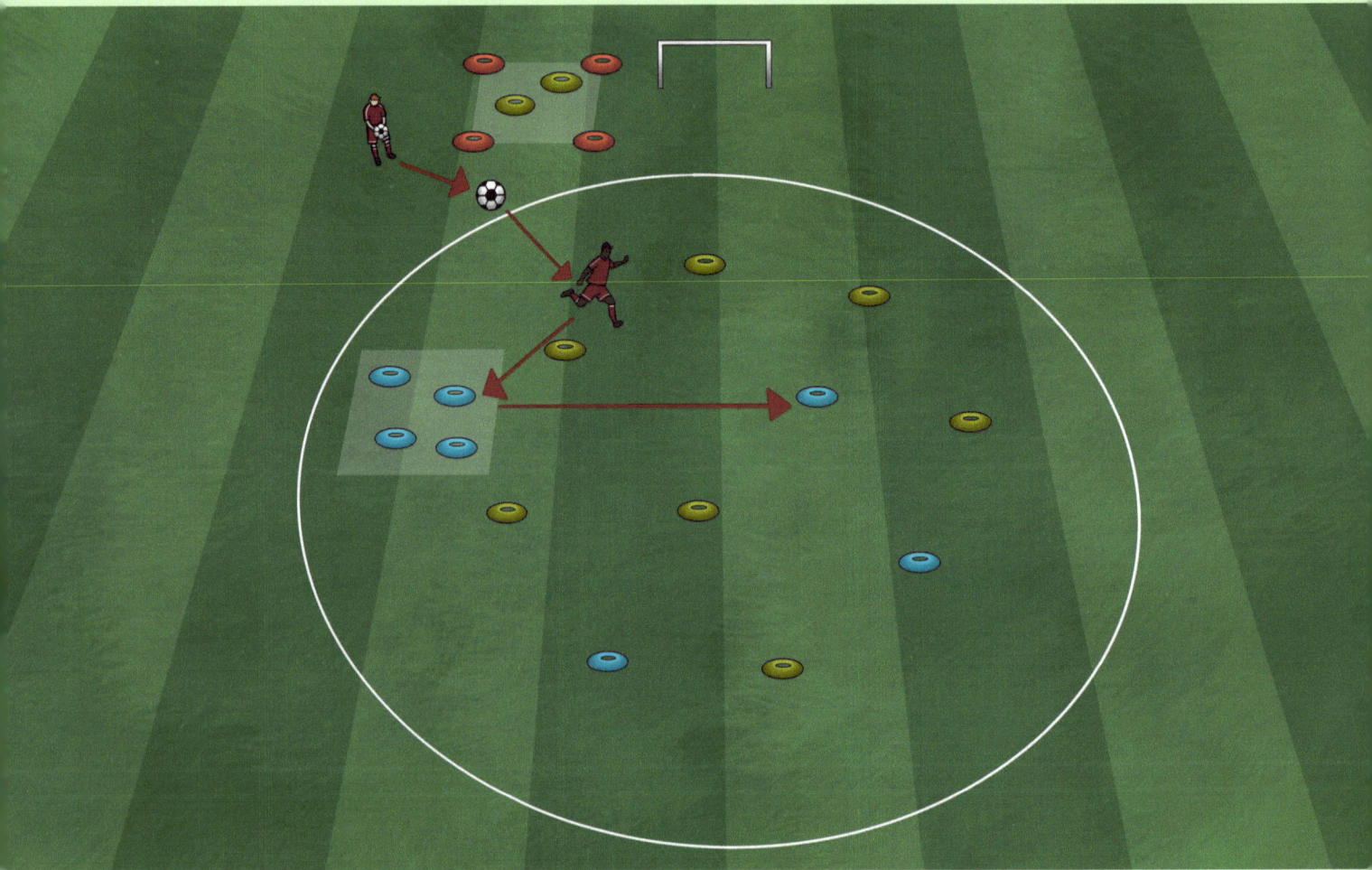

BURY THE TREASURE

Organisation of Game

Place rocks (cones) on Treasure Island.

Pirates take the treasure from the treasure chest (all the cones) and load it onto their pirate ships.

Pirates sail their pirate ships (hold the balls) back to Treasure Island.

Pirates dock their pirate ships (place the balls on the ground) and climb onto Treasure Island.

Pirates scatter the treasure (cones) on the ground.

Pirates collect a rock (cone) and place it over the treasure to bury it.

Progression

Pirates place the balls on the ground and dribble across the ocean using little kicks.

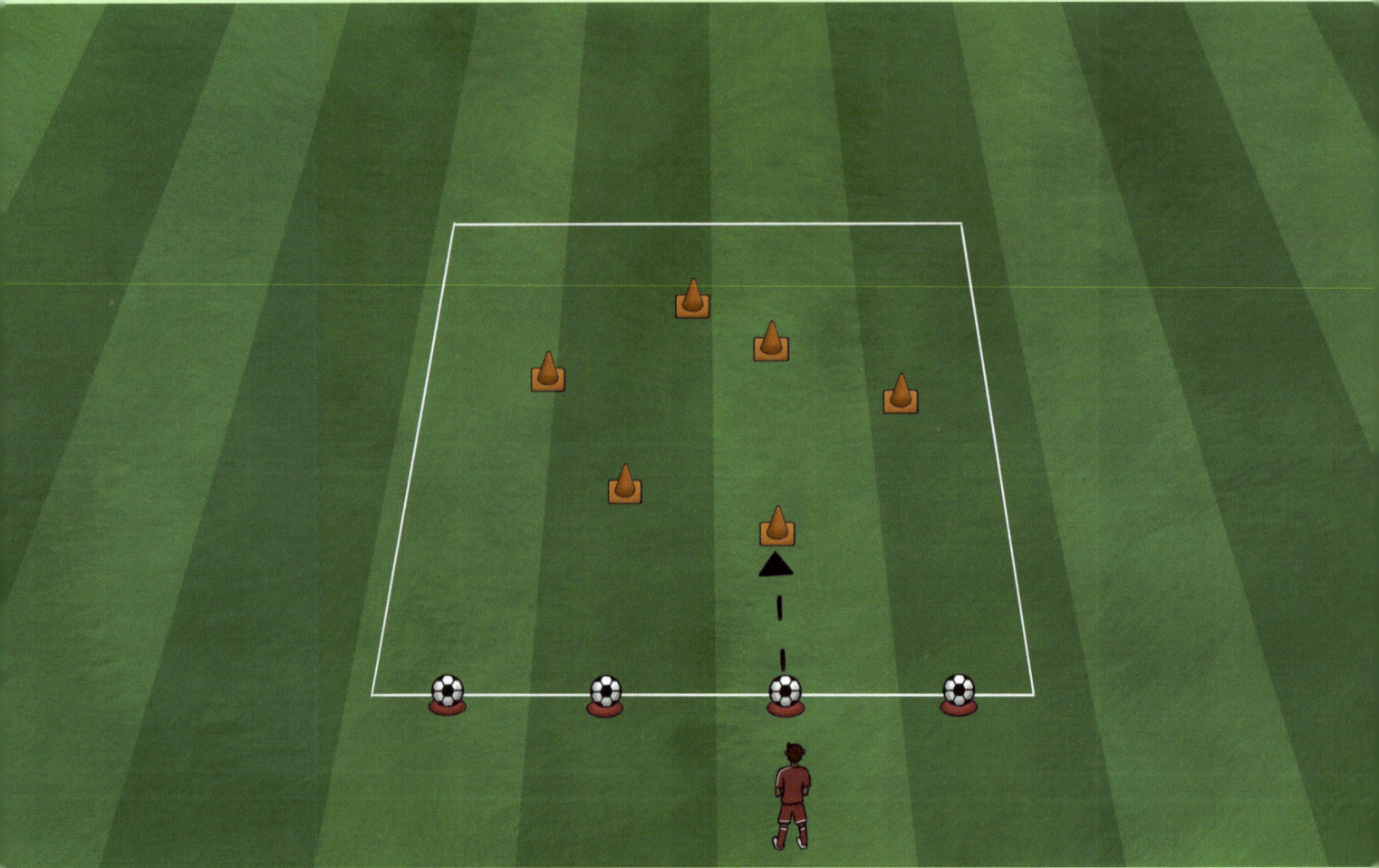

STOP THE PIRATES

Organisation of Game

Create the side of a pirate ship using cones.

Place cannons (cones) along the edge of the pirate ship.

Place cannonballs into the cannons (balls on top of the cones).

Place naughty pirate ships (tall cones) out at sea (at a suitable distance from the pirate ship).

Pirates fire (kick the balls) the cannons at the pirate ships to sink them (knock them down).

Pirates attempt to stop the naughty pirates by sinking all the pirate ships.

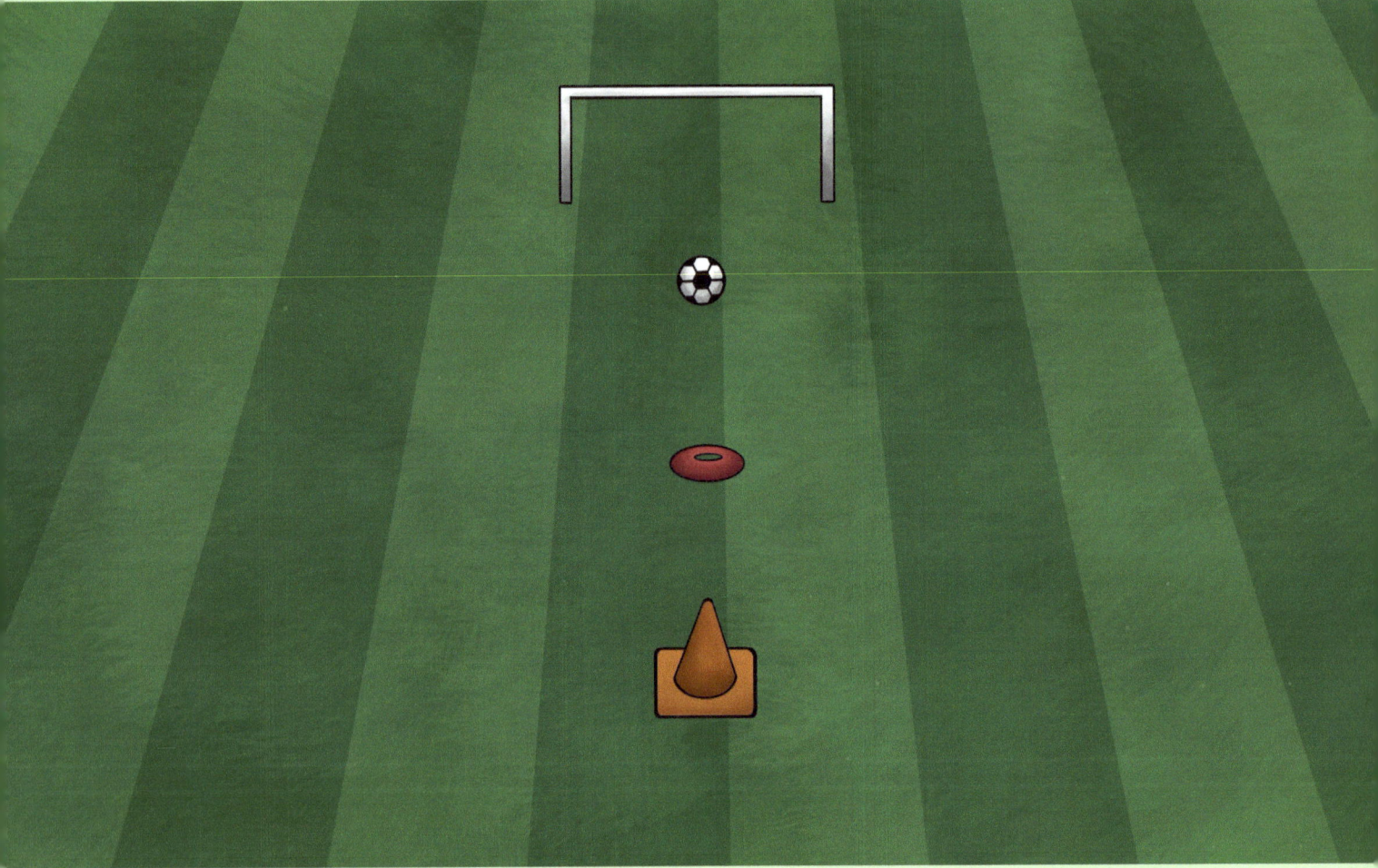

EQUIPMENT REQUIRED

If the suggested equipment is unavailable, you can be creative!

Can you find something in the house or garden to use instead?

Instead of a goal, you could use jumpers as goal posts.

Instead of a football, you could use any round object.

Instead of cones, you could use rocks.

Instead of tall cones, you could use tins of baked beans.

AUTHOR PROFILE

Tom Oldaker holds a MSc in Sports Coaching, a PGCE in PE teaching and has previously worked within education and the sports coaching sectors. He specialises in the grassroots and development phases, coaching and teaching of children aged 2-11 in the UK, Australia, India and Bahrain.

Alongside his passion for creativity, learning and child development, this book was inspired by delivering football coaching sessions to 2-6-year-olds, focusing on the holistic development of the child through fun games. After years of modifying and animating games to make them more fun and engaging for learners, sessions were produced to allow children the opportunity to play characters within a story. Having refined this story, he decided to share it with children around the world, giving them the chance to bring the story to life while also facilitating their holistic development.

WHAT DID YOU THINK OF:

THE ADVENTURES OF ALEX THE PIRATE: TREASURE ISLAND?

A big thank you for purchasing this book. It means a lot that you chose this book specifically from such a wide range on offer. I do hope you enjoyed it.

Book reviews are incredibly important for an author. All feedback helps them improve their writing for future projects and for developing this edition. If you are able to spare a few minutes to post a review on Amazon, that would be much appreciated.

Publisher Information

rowanvale
books

Rowanvale Books provides publishing services to independent authors, writers and poets all over the globe. We deliver a personal, honest and efficient service that allows authors to see their work published, while remaining in control of the process and retaining their creativity. By making publishing services available to authors in a cost-effective and ethical way, we at Rowanvale Books hope to ensure that the local, national and international community benefits from a steady stream of good quality literature.

For more information about us, our authors or our publications, please get in touch.
www.rowanvalebooks.com
info@rowanvalebooks.com

www.ingramcontent.com/pod-product-compliance
Lightning Source LLC
Chambersburg PA
CBHW042108040426
42448CB00002B/189